A guide
Gower Peninsula
Swansea

Clare Gogerty

National Trust

Sir Karl Jenkins' Gower	2
Gower: A Brief History	4
Smugglers, shipwrecks and saving the coast	6
A timeline of National Trust ownership	8
A poet's place: Dylan Thomas and Vernon Watkins	10
Touring the Coast	12
Bishopston Valley and Pwlldu Bay	14
🚶 Bishopston Valley	16
Pennard Cliffs	18
🚶 Southgate, Hunts Bay and Pwlldu circular walk	20
Three Cliffs Bay	22
Three Cliffs Bay: castles, coast and kilns	24
🚶 Three Cliffs Bay and Pennard Cliffs	26
Nicholaston Burrows and Oxwich Bay	28
🚶 Nicholaston Bay circular walk	30
The South Coast	32
Areas of South Gower	34
Fall Bay	34
Thurba Bay	34
Port Eynon	34
The mystery of Paviland Cave	35
Culver Hole	36
Rhossili Down	38
Highlights of Rhossili Down	40
Rhossili Bay	42
🚶 Rhossili Down, Hillend and Rhossili beach	44
Worms Head	46
🚶 Serpents, seascapes and shipwrecks	48
The Vile	50
Whiteford Burrows	52
Around Whiteford Burrows	54
Llanmadoc Hill, Ryers Down and Cheriton	54
Cwm Ivy	54
🚶 Llanmadoc Green to Berges Island	56
The North Coast	58
Llanrhidian Marsh and the estuary	60
Looking after Gower	62
The changing coastline and Cwm Ivy	62
Plans for the future	64

Sir Karl Jenkins' Gower
Hafan i gyfansoddwr

'The Gower Peninsula is my home. Although essentially London based since I came to the Royal Academy of Music in 1966, and while I travel extensively with my music, I return to Gower regularly and for nearly all my 70 years I've had a dwelling there.

I was raised and educated at Gower as a schoolboy and my family is buried there. We lived in the coastal village of Penclawdd, famous for its cockles, which is situated on the northern side of this 70-square-mile peninsula that projects westward into the Bristol Channel. I have always thought that what gives Gower its special character is that, like all peninsulas, it is three-quarters of the way to being an island.

A magical and intriguing place, the Gower Peninsula was the first part of the United Kingdom to be officially designated an Area of Outstanding Natural Beauty. Pretty much rectangular in shape, it boasts 17 churches (many going back 800 years) and several castles. The western coast of the 'rectangle' is occupied,

Above Looking north from Ryers Down, one of the places Sir Karl Jenkins could see when writing from his 'stable block'

pretty much solely, by the three-mile stretch of iconic Rhossili Bay, which often wins 'best beach' awards in the UK and even Europe.

One could almost draw a line from the northwest corner to Swansea in the southeast; south of that line is a land of agriculture and farming with sandy beaches, dramatic cliff scenery with coastal caves. In one such cave was found the Red Lady of Paviland, one of the oldest human skeletons ever discovered, while Parc Le Breos, a burial chamber, was built c.6000BC. Atop Cefn Bryn stands King Arthur's stone, a Bronze Age standing stone. Local legend has it that it was a stone in Arthur's shoe that he threw, from Camelot, over the Bristol Channel to Gower!

The north overlooks the flat marshes of the Bury Estuary, where the cockles are gathered, and which had a more industrial past, particularly toward the east.

As a composer, Gower was always an inspirational place. For many years I wrote from a 'stable block', enjoying a vista of the Bury Pill river valley across to Ryers Down, all of which was once part of a pre-Norman medieval Welsh 'maenor'. Even though I have written a great deal of music away from Gower, the soul of the place comes with me, as a friend, as a haven, lending succor and evoking memories.'

Sir Karl Jenkins,
Composer

Gower: A Brief History
Cip ar hanes Bro Gŵyr

The history of Gower is written in its landscape. Traces of its past – from prehistoric burial chambers to a Second World War radar station – are there for all to discover.

Much of this is governed by the peninsula's topography: bones of a Paleolithic man are hidden inside a cave; a medieval field system survives on fertile free-draining soil; Iron Age fortifications are positioned on towering headlands; a ship wrecked on jagged rocks is stranded on a wind-blown beach.

The land
Gower's diverse landscape – saltmarsh, sandy beaches, rocky caves, grassland and cliffs – is the result of what lies beneath it. The base layer of much of it, Old Red Sandstone, was formed 400 million years ago, during the Devonian period. Movement of the earth caused this to ruck up, creating hills and valleys. Sea levels rose as the climate changed, submerging most of the land beneath tropical water. Skeletons of coral and other marine creatures silted to the bottom, eventually forming a layer of carboniferous limestone which is the bedrock of most of Gower. The high ground of Cefn Bryn, Rhossili Down, Ryers Down and Harding's Down are all Old Devonian Red Sandstone. South Gower, however, lies on top of limestone.

The people
Gower's fertile ground and sheltered caves have been inhabited by man for over 26,000 years. Evidence of early occupation is everywhere, from Bronze Age menhirs (standing stones) – most notably, Arthur's Stone on Cefn Bryn – to Neolithic chambered tombs such as Sweynes Howes on Rhossili Down. Iron Age hill forts and cairns pepper hilltops. In the 19th century, the renowned Red Lady of Paviland was discovered in Goat's Hole cave (see page 35).

Left Arthur's Stone that sits on Cefn Bryn, sometimes known as King Arthur's Stone or *Maen Ceti*. It dates back to 2500BC and was one of the first sites to be protected under the 1882 Ancient Monuments Act

Right top A Gower potato farm photographed in July 1951

Right centre Picking potatoes on Tom Beynon's farm in Gower, July 1963

Right bottom An early bus at Gower

Far right A lookout tower on Llanrhidian Marsh hints to the area's military past

Agricultural roots

Farming has always been at the heart of the community. Until the arrival of tractors here in 1930, traditional agricultural practices continued relatively unchanged for centuries with the majority of the population working on the land. Those who didn't worked in the limestone quarries along the south coast or in Penclawdd's tin and copper mines or, more recently, commuted to Swansea.

The Second World War

Being remote and relatively uninhabited, Gower was the ideal location to test artillery during the Second World War. A test range was established at Crofty, to the north of the peninsula. Guns fired explosive and non-explosive shells into the sand and mud daily. Also tested was an anthrax bomb; on 28 October 1942, this was dropped on 60 sheep tethered on the sand. Two of the sheep were contaminated and the test was considered a success.

A radar station was also installed on Rhossili Down. Originally intended to monitor shipping and low-flying aircraft, it was updated in 1942 and became part of a group of radar stations covering the Bristol Channel. It closed in 1945 and was dismantled, leaving only the concrete foundations.

Mae dylanwad daeareg yn drwm ar ddyn a byd natur ym Mro Gŵyr – y tywodfaen coch a gododd yn fryniau dros 400 miliwn o flynyddoedd yn ôl, a'r haen o gwrel a chregyn a ffurfiodd uwch ei ben wedi i'r môr orlifo'r tir. Hyn sy'n cyfrif am y gwahanol gynefinoedd sy'n nodweddu Gŵyr. Dyma'r allwedd hefyd i hanes pobl ar y pentir: o'r ogofâu a'u hesgyrn cyn-oesol, y meini hirion a'r beddrodau hynafol i'r amaethu, y pysgota a'r mwyngloddio fu'n rhan mor ganolog o fywyd dros y canrifoedd. Topograffeg y penrhyn oedd y rheswm dros ei ddewis fel safle i brofi arfau ac i wylio llongau ac awyrennau ym Môr Hafren yn ystod yr 2il Ryfel Byd.

GOWER: A BRIEF HISTORY 5

Smugglers, shipwrecks and saving the coast
Trasiedi a thrysor ar hyd y glannau

This page The shipwrecked remains of *The Helvetia* on Rhossili beach

Opposite An advert for the auctioning of goods from a wrecked ship in 1876

No point on Gower is further than two-and-a-half miles from the sea. Poking out into the Atlantic Ocean and situated at the head of the Bristol Channel, it is not surprising that sea faring has been integral to the fortunes of its people.

The smugglers

With its secluded coves and inlets, Gower's south coast was perfect territory for smugglers. During the 18th century, this was a well-organised business with big money made from the illegal importation of contraband from the Channel Islands and France – Swansea Customs House estimated no fewer than 5,000 kegs of liquor were brought ashore in the six-month period to August 1795. Contraband was hidden in caves before armed criminal gangs whisked it away under cover of darkness – and under the noses of custom officers.

Locals allegedly sometimes used more devious methods to trick officers. It is said that one cold morning, a local housewife provided a pair with plenty of tea and brandy, but the water in the kettle was actually hot gin. The officers drank so much they became too drunk and drowsy to realise the neighbours were frantically dispersing the village store of contraband.

The demise of smuggling came in the early 19th century: in the 1820s the Royal Navy began to blockade smugglers' ships, later with the aid of the Coastguard.

Fishing roots

More legitimately, fishing from the Port Eynon harbour has sustained inhabitants and cockle picking is still a profitable business at Penclawdd (see page 61).

Treacherous waters

The combination of dangerous currents, ferocious winds and a rocky shoreline led, inevitably, to shipwrecks along Gower's coastline during the 18th and 19th centuries – over 250 ships were wrecked or stranded here. St Mary's Church at Rhossili even has a dedicated corner in the churchyard for dead sailors. These wrecks provided booty for local villagers when wine, fruit, silver dollars, ivory and coal, and even live pigs, turned up on the beaches.

Evidence of some of these wrecks can still be seen at Gower, including *The Helvetia*, a sailing ship that fell victim to a storm on 1 November 1887 and which now lies on Rhossili beach. The crew was rescued by means of a rocket fired to the stranded ship from a trailer towed by a horse or lorry. The rocket carried a line that the crew used to haul a longer, stronger line known as the whip, from which was suspended a canvas harness (a breeches buoy). This was used to haul the crew to safety one by one. The ship and its cargo of timber were thrown ashore by the waves; its bow has remained here ever since.

WRECK SALE.
PAVILAND, GOWER.

Messrs. EDWARD ROBEETS & SON Have been instructed on behalf of the Underwriters, TO SELL BY PUBLIC AUCTION, On the Beach under Paviland and along the Coast, On MONDAY, JANUARY 3, 1876,

THE whole of the Cargo saved from the wreck of the barque Jenny, from Pensacola, consisting of about 500 LOGS OF SAWN PITCH PINE TIMBER, in lengths from 20 feet to 45 feet by about 1 foot square. For further particulars apply to Mr. George Gibbs, Lloyd's Agent, Port Eynon; or to the Auctioneers, 6, Picton-place, Swansea.

Sale to commence at Twelve o'clock.—Terms cash.

Mae'r môr wedi dod â'i siâr o gyfoeth a galar i Benrhyn Gŵyr. Roedd smyglo a gwreca yn rhan o fywyd yr ardal yn y 18fed a'r 19egG; cai gwirodydd eu mewnforio'n gyfrinachol dan drwynau Swyddogion y Tollau, ac roedd trigolion yn heidio i'r traethau i gasglu arian, pren, ffrwythau, gwin, ifori a glo yn dilyn llongddryllliadau. Mae 'sgerbwd un o'r llongau anffodus hyn, *The Helvetia*, i'w weld o hyd ar draeth Rhosili.

A timeline of National Trust ownership
Degawdau o ofal

The National Trust has been committed to looking after Gower since 1933, when Thurba Head was given into our care.

We now manage 26 miles of the Gower coastline – three-quarters of its total – ensuring that it remains unspoiled and available for everyone to enjoy, forever.

1933
The Trust is given Thurba Head, south of Rhossili

1954
Given Bishopston Valley, Pwlldu, Kittle Green and much of Pennard Cliffs

1955
Given Notthill

1956
Gower is declared an Area of Outstanding Natural Beauty by the National Parks Commission after much pressure by The Gower Society

1964–67
The Trust acquires Overton Mere and Culver Hole

1965
Enterprise Neptune, the National Trust's campaign to save the coast, is launched. The National Trust buys Whiteford Burrows

Given Cwm Ivy, including The Lodge. This had to be knocked down and rebuilt in 2012

A view towards the beach and dunes at Whiteford Burrows

Acquires 17 miles of coast and a number of inland sites from the Penrice Estate, including: Cefn Bryn, Landimore Marsh, Llanrhidian Marsh, Nicholaston Beach and Burrows, Oxwich Bay, Penmaen Burrows, Rhossili Down and Cliffs, Three Cliffs, Tor Bay, Ryers Down and Worms Head

1967

The first part of the Vile comes under National Trust protection

1988

Buys the car park in Rhossili Village

2015

1981

Acquires the first of the three Coastguard Cottages (the others were acquired in 1982 and 2000)

1995

The National Trust buys The Old Rectory, a cottage dating from the 1850s, on Rhossili Down and lets it out as holiday accommodation

A poet's place: Dylan Thomas and Vernon Watkins
Bro Beirdd

'Gower is a very beautiful peninsula, some miles from this blowsy town and so far the Tea-Shop philistines have not spoilt the more beautiful of its bays … as a matter of fact it is one of the loveliest sea-coast stretches in the whole of Britain.' So proclaimed poet Dylan Thomas of Gower in 1933, writing to his then-girlfriend, Pamela Hansford Johnson.

One of Wales' most renowned literary figures, Thomas (1914–53) was Swansea born and bred. As he grew older, he often headed to Rhossili on the bus and regularly camped there with friends in summer.

Gower in Thomas's work

One of these trips features in 'Who Do You Wish Was With Us?', a short story taken from Thomas's autobiographical book *A Portrait of the Artist as a Young Dog*. It details the occasion on which Thomas and a friend became stranded on Worms Head after misjudging the speed of the tide.

Gower also features in another short story by Thomas, 'Extraordinary Little Cough':

'Laughing on the cliff above the very long golden beach, we pointed out to each other, as though the other were blind, the great rock of the Worms Head. The sea was out. We crossed over on slipping stones and stood, at last, triumphantly on the windy top. There was monstrous thick grass there that made us spring-heeled and we laughed and bounced on it, scaring the sheep who ran up and down the battered sides like goats. Even on this calmest day a wind blew on the Worm.'

Below Dylan Thomas, photographed by John Gay and published in July 1948

Vernon Watkins

Dylan Thomas was not the only writer to have been inspired by Gower. The area also features in poems by Vernon Watkins (1906–67), a good friend of Thomas's, and described as 'One of the most distinguished poets of our time' (*The Spectator*, 1967).

Watkins' family settled on the Gower Peninsula during his youth and he lived here for most of his life, mainly at Pennard. 'He knew every yard of the Gower slades with the precision of a naturalist' read his obituary in *The Spectator* (1967).

During his lifetime, Watkins published eight volumes of poetry with Faber (a ninth was published posthumously), and was apparently being considered for Poet Laureate at the time of his death.

> Dau fardd eingl-Gymraeg enwog a ysbrydolwyd gan Benrhyn Gŵyr oedd Dylan Thomas a Vernon Watkins. Mae eu disgrifiadau manwl a thelynegol o'r amgylchedd naturiol, ac o'u profiadau o fyw a chrwydro yn yr ardal, yn adlewyrchu eu hoffter o'r fro hon.

Top left Vernon Watkins' memorial stone at Pennard Cliffs, Hunts Bay. It features lines from his poem 'Taliesin in Gower'

Above A letter from Dylan Thomas to Vernon Watkins

Touring the Coast
Pen draw'r byd ar drothwy'r ddinas

Tucked away on the South Wales coast, Gower is not on the road to anywhere.

You have to know about it to visit, but once you do, you are sure to come back. It is, as journalist and broadcaster Wynford Vaughan Thomas once said described, 'a secret that people hug to themselves'.

This section is a guide to some of the places you might explore while you're here – or during a future visit.

Right Sea holly and grass on the side of a sand dune at Whiteford Burrows

Bishopston Valley and Pwlldu Bay

Cysgodion ddoe mewn cwm coediog

The National Trust bought most of Bishopston Valley and nearby Pennard Cliffs (see page 18) in 1954 to protect the area from development (the remainder was gifted to us in 1963).

The area is now designated a Site of Special Scientific Interest (SSSI) and Special Area of Conservation. The woods date to the 17th century, when the whole of Gower would have been covered by trees. Under ownership of the Trust, trees, scrubland and meadows have been managed to encourage diversification of plant and animal life. Birds, insects, fungi and woodland plants have all flourished as a result. Dippers, herons, little egrets, kingfishers and yellow wagtails are often seen along the banks of the Bishopston stream, and trees such as the wild service tree and the small-leaved lime have become established.

Mining in the valley

Before Bishopston Valley became an important conservation area, it was an industrial landscape: silver and lead were mined here until 1854. The remains of Long Ash Mine and the houses of the miners who worked there can still be seen, but are now home to greater and lesser horseshoe bats, who come here to roost.

Pwlldu

The beach at Pwlldu is not the easiest to reach; there is no convenient car park at its edge. Instead it is best approached by a 4-mile (6km) walk, through ancient woodland banked along a narrow limestone valley and its meandering stream (see page 16).

Emerging from the woody, sheltered valley into Pwlldu Bay is a glorious moment. At low tide, the beach opens up to the sea before you. The 90-metre (295-foot) high Pwlldu Head at its western end protects the bay from winds and rough currents, creating a safe and peaceful place to swim (although be aware that there is no lifeguard on patrol and the currents around the headland are dangerous).

'Pwlldu' means 'black pool' in Welsh. It refers to the pool of water behind a bank of pebbles piled into a ridge by the actions of waves and wind during stormy weather. Most of these pebbles were created by limestone quarrying at the west side of the bay during the early part of the 19th century. Demand for limestone from building and agriculture was high and met by large stones being quarried by blasting or chiselling and then dragged to the water's edge where they were broken into smaller pieces and piled into heaps on the beach. Most limestone was exported to North Devon, a practice that continued until 1902. At the height of the quarrying, up to thirty boats might have been seen in the bay at any one time.

A smuggler's paradise
In the second half of the 18th century, Pwlldu Bay was a favoured smuggling spot. Once hauled ashore, contraband could be taken up the wooded Bishopston Valley to be sold in the markets of nearby Swansea. Pwlldu Head provided a convenient look-out post to guide boats to the bay at its foot and to stave off customs men. It has been said that at this time more contraband was landed here than anywhere else in the Bristol Channel.

⊙ LOOK OUT FOR

Little egret
The small white heron is often spied along the banks of Bishopston stream.

Wild service tree (*Sorbus torminalis*)
This rare specimen is only seen in areas of ancient woodland.

Above Snow melting in Bishopston Valley

Left Little egrets are a common sight in Wales, as well as on the south and east coasts of England

Far left Pwlldu Bay, one of Gower's most secluded beaches

arian coedwig **ystlumod** nant **crëyr bach** pisgwydden plwm **calchfaen** llyncdwll **chwarel** cerddinen wyllt

TOURING THE COAST 15

🚶 WALK THIS WAY
Bishopston Valley
Porth i draeth perta'r byd

Discover a secret world of limestone caves, underground rivers and ancient woodland, before emerging from beneath the canopy onto one of Gower's most beautiful, but secluded, beaches.

- Moderate
- 2 hours 30 mins
- 4 miles/6.4km
- Dog friendly

Terrain: a challenging walk through a wooded valley, including muddy woodland floors and an uneven stony path. The walk starts with a steep descent into the valley and ends at a beach with a pebble ridge.

🏴 Mae disgrifiad Cymraeg o'r daith hon ar ein gwefan

Starting point: Kittle Green

1. Starting at Kittle Green, walk past the National Trust sign. Keeping Great Kittle farm on your right, follow the footpath into the trees. The path drops down the slope for about ¼ miles (0.4km) and can be slippery after rain. When you reach a fork in the path, bear left and go down the steps until you reach the chestnut fence on your right. The enormous hole in the ground is called Daw Pit. This was formed where the underground river caused land to collapse.

2. Continue down the steep slope to the bottom and turn right along the dry river bed. Cross the river to walk on the left hand side, taking care on the uneven surface for about 200yds (180m). The track crosses back across the river at this point. During wet periods the river will be running, but it is usually shallow and easily crossed. The stream sometimes disappears into holes called 'sinks' and re-emerges halfway down the valley to run above ground.

3. The track here is usually muddy. Keep listening for the sound of the river as you get closer to Guzzle Hole, a cave. From the outside you can hear water thundering in the underground stream, often making unusual sounds, hence the name 'guzzle'.

4. Long Ash Mine can be seen on your left. The mine produced both silver and lead and was in service until 1854. The grille is in place to protect the roosts of greater and lesser horseshoe bats. There are also remains of old miners' cottages nearby.

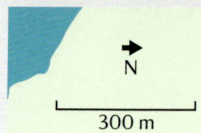

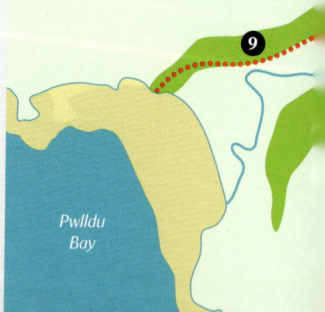

5. Cross the river again and go up some steps, keeping left.

6. You will soon come across one of three bridges that cross the river along the valley. The valley was once a busy place providing food, fuel and work for many surrounding villages and a number of small footpaths still link communities to the wood. Do not cross the bridge but continue on the path alongside the river. Look out for the old stone walls on your right as you continue, remnants from when the valley was grazed and there were fewer trees than there are now.

7. Follow the path into the meadow in front of you. The wet meadows in the valley are registered as common land and are home to a number of wildflowers. Follow the path as it heads back out of the meadow and resumes its place alongside the river. Soon you will reach another bridge. Do not cross it; instead continue along the path until you reach a fork.

8. At the fork in the path, keep left. Soon you will come to a right turn in the path. Continue straight ahead, keeping the river alongside the path following the sign to Pwlldu Bay.

9. Go past the fence on the edge of the path. Where it forks, follow the path left down the hill. Do not cross the bridge. When you reach the private garden, turn left and walk onto the beach.

Top Pwlldu Bay at sunset

Far left Look out for the rare wild service tree during your walk – the trees can grow up to 25 metres (82 feet)

TOURING THE COAST 17

Pennard Cliffs
Bedd morwyr ac eliffantod

The two-mile stretch of cliffs between Pwlldu Head and Three Cliffs Bay offers one of the most all-encompassing views on Gower. Walk along the clifftop path on a clear, bright day and you will have views along the south coast of the peninsula around to Oxwich Point and across the Bristol Channel to Devon.

The National Trust acquired Pennard Cliffs in 1954 to prevent the creep of residential development. This is common land and local farmers still exercise their ancient rights and graze their sheep here. The cropping of the grass and the dropping of manure plays an important part in conserving the plant life and has led to an abundance of wild flowers. Birds, including choughs and ravens, also thrive here and can often be spotted from the cliffs.

Caves in the cliffs

Gower's limestone cliffs are frequently perforated with caves which tunnel into the cliff face, some for several metres. Two of the largest can be found in Pennard Cliffs: Bacon Hole and Minchin Hole. Bacon Hole is so named because of the dark red streaks along its walls, which caused considerable excitement when the cave was first excavated in 1912. Originally it was thought that the streaks were part of some sort of prehistoric art but later investigations revealed the markings to be red oxide seeping through the rock. Archaeological finds at both Bacon and Minchin Hole include the remains of several extinct animals including the straight-tusked elephant and soft-nosed rhinoceros. Today the only thing you will find in the caves are bats.

Graves End

In 1760 a naval vessel, *Caesar,* was wrecked on the rocks off Pennard Cliffs. Many of the sailors on board had been press-ganged into recruitment and were locked below deck. When the ship foundered on the rocks, its passengers perished also. They were buried in a mass grave on the clifftop called, fittingly, Graves End.

What are commons?

The National Trust owns 1,760 hectares (4,349 acres) of common land on Gower, including Pennard Cliffs. Common land dates back centuries to when local people were given the right to fish, collect firewood, and graze animals on pieces of land of no use to the Lord of the Manor. This continuing practice of grazing and burning has created a rich tapestry of habitats including heathland and wetland which are important for the conservation of wildlife and plants. *For more information: gowercommons.org.uk.*

Above The beach at Pennard

Right Yellow whitlow grass is a dainty wildflower that can only be seen at Gower. The best time to see it is March–May

Far right The red, bacon-fat-like streaks inside Bacon Hole

llongddrylliad tir comin **brain coesgoch** *Caesar* **rhinoseros** caer llysiau'r-bystwn melyn **bedd morwyr** eliffant **ogofâu** ystlumod **cigfrain**

✓ THINGS TO DO AT PENNARD

Clamber into Bacon Cave
Explore its two chambers, which extend 45 metres (147 feet) into the cliff face.

Explore High Pennard, an Iron Age promontory fort
Look out for ditches and banks of earth that were once the home of people from the first and second centuries AD.

Take a sketchbook
Try to capture the spectacular scenery in front of you.

Walk the clifftop path
See if you can spot the shoreline of Devon across the Bristol Channel.

◉ LOOK OUT FOR

Bats
Many of the caves on the south coast of Gower are home to a variety of bats including the greater horseshoe, lesser horseshoe, whiskered and pipistrelle.

Yellow whitlow grass
This stretch of the south Gower coast is the only place this pretty yellow flower – which is also the county flower of Swansea – grows in the UK.

WALK THIS WAY

Southgate, Hunts Bay and Pwlldu circular walk
Caer hen a llecyn claddu

A walk for wildlife lovers. This stretch of coastline is particularly important for plants that flourish in limestone grassland and it's the only place in the UK where the yellow whitlow grass grows.

 Moderate

 2 hours

 4 miles/6.4km

 Dog friendly

Terrain: varied from clifftop paths and stony tracks to woodland paths (often muddy). Some of the route is steep. There are stiles and steps.

🏴 Mae disgrifiad Cymraeg o'r daith hon ar ein gwefan

Start: National Trust car park, Southgate

1. With the National Trust car park hut on your right, walk along the track for about a mile (1.6km). On a clear day there are spectacular views across the Bristol Channel to Somerset and Devon.

2. When you reach Hunts Farm, fork right on to the coast path, signed Pwlldu Head. This will go up some steps, with a wall on your left.

3. When you pass a small pond on your left, look for the path which bears right and go uphill with a fence on the left. When you reach the top, look out for the banks and ditches – all that remains of an Iron Age promontory fort.

4. Continue along the coast path, following the route through the gorse and around the headland.

5. You are now standing on a cliff known as Graves End, so named as it's near the spot where the ship *Caesar* was wrecked in 1760 (see page 18).

6. Follow the path back to the car park.

High Pennard is one of a series of Iron Age promontory forts irregularly spaced along the South Gower coast. Pottery dating to the first or second century AD has been found here.

Right A walker enjoying Pennard Cliffs

Far right A view east along the Pennard coastline and Pwlldu Bay

Three Cliffs Bay
Trysor o fae

Three Cliffs Bay is not the most accessible beach on Gower – you will need to park the car and follow the footpath to the beach – but it is well worth the effort.

If you approach from the clifftop, you will understand why this area is so photographed. A wide bay of sand opens up before you, lined with ragged rocks, a natural arch and sea-bashed coves. The bay's name comes from the three tooth-like, pointed cliffs that jut into the sea at its eastern edge.

Turn to page 24 for an in-depth look at the many areas of Three Cliffs Bay there are to discover.

'To me, Three Cliffs always feels so intimate and cosy. It gives me the feeling of being hugged … every time [I visit] I'm struck by the magic of it again. It still takes my breath away.'

Katherine Jenkins, writing in *The Sunday Times*

Top Sunset at Three Cliffs Bay; the peaks after which it's named are visible in the foreground

Right Choughs are spotted along rocky coasts with short grassland. There are 250–350 breeding pairs in the UK

👁 LOOK OUT FOR

Choughs
With their distinctive red legs and beak and jet black bodies, these birds are often seen on the common land on the cliffs where sheep graze. A welcome sight, choughs have returned to Gower after an absence of nearly one hundred years.

22 TOURING THE COAST

*Yng nghesail bae, yng nghysgod nos,
aur y dydd sy'n aros.*

✓ THINGS TO DO AT THREE CLIFFS BAY

Climb a cliff
The three 20-metre (66-foot) high limestone cliffs after which the bay is named are a popular destination for rock climbers. They are a challenge that should be tackled by experienced climbers only.

Pitch a tent
The local campsite has spectacular views – unzip your tent in the morning and boil a kettle looking out over the bay.

Ride on the beach
Local stables have horses that will take you trekking on the sand.

Star gaze
The skies above Gower are clear enough to see many different constellations. Turn your telescope to the west, over the British Channel, for the best results.

Stay on land
There are strong rip tides and currents in the bay and no lifeguards, so swimming and watersports are not encouraged.

Walk the dog
Dogs are allowed all year round at Three Cliffs Bay. Bring a Frisbee, too, for added lung-filling pleasure.

Left Rock climbing is a popular activity at Three Cliffs, but should only be attempted by experienced climbers with the correct equipment

TOURING THE COAST 23

Three Cliffs Bay: castles, coast and kilns
Llinyn arian trwy dywod aur

From ancient history to bays and beaches, there's a lot to discover at Three Cliffs Bay.

The shoreline
At low tide, follow the course of Pennard Pill. The large stream meanders towards the sea, past Pennard Castle on the hillside above it, through the middle of Three Cliffs Bay, to the shoreline. Afterwards, explore the two different but secluded beaches on either side: Pobbles Bay to the east is surrounded by limestone cliffs. To the west (on the other side of Great Tor, see below), Tor Bay has a large u-shaped beach and is partially sheltered. Both are good places to throw down a rug and enjoy a sandwich. Although separated at high tide, you can walk between them when the sea recedes.

Ancient remains
For the best views, approach Three Cliffs Bay with a walk across Penmaen Burrows, a grassy headland on top of the 60-metre (197-foot) high cliffs. At its centre is a large megalithic tomb, Pen-y-Crug, believed to be 5,000 years old and evidence of one of the first communities on Gower. Nearby, banks of earth are all that remain of the ringwork (circular entrenchment) of a 12th-century Norman castle. Other traces of the Norman settlement include a man-made rabbit warren known as Pillow Mound, built to provide villagers with a source of food. At the end of the headland is Great Tor, a precipitous limestone rock face popular with climbers. Prehistoric animal bones have been found in Leather's Hole Cave at its base.

Notthill
Further inland, Notthill is two hectares (five acres) of recovering heathland that comes alive with bluebells in spring. Notthill was saved from development by Miss E R Lee in 1955. The land had been divided into building lots, all of which she bought and presented to the National Trust. The Trust has continued to manage it ever since, particularly keeping the bracken and gorse under control to enable a wide range of heathland plants to re-establish, and opening up access for visitors.

Pennard Castle
High on the hill overlooking Three Cliffs Bay, the small, romantic ruin of Pennard Castle (not National Trust) makes a Gothic silhouette, especially as the light fades at dusk. Commissioned in the 12th century by the Earl of Warwick, it was originally a wooden building. The timber structure was replaced by a limestone and sandstone one in the 13th century. However, this was unable to withstand the battering of sand whipped up by the wind and had fallen into ruin by the 14th century.

clychau'r gog cerrig camu **cwningar** beddrod **dringwyr** castell **calchfaen** Pen y Crug bwa craig **esgyrn** odyn galch **storm dywod** **brain coesgoch** cefn draig

Lime kilns

As you walk through Penmaen Burrows, keep an eye open for a restored double-fronted lime kiln. Lime kilns were seen along the south Gower coast until 1900 when they were used to extract lime from limestone for agriculture and building. Much of this was exported to Devon and had three principle uses: to spread on soil to increase its fertility; for use in mortar for construction; and as a limewash applied to the exterior of buildings. When they were in operation, the kilns burned with a blue flame and gave off a thick yellow smoke which could be seen by boats all along the coastline.

Left The view to Three Cliffs Bay from Penmaen

Above A lime kiln on the path from Penmaen down to Tor Bay. The path to the right leads to Nicholaston Woods and Oxwich Bay

TOURING THE COAST 25

🚶 WALK THIS WAY

Three Cliffs Bay and Pennard Cliffs
O lawr dyffryn i ben clogwyn

Take in the spectacular views over Gower and South Pembrokeshire, before picnicking on one of Gower's most well-known beaches. There's also the option to go a little further in pursuit of views of Pennard Castle.

- Moderate
- 30 minutes
- 1 mile/1.6km
- Dog friendly

Please note: Although dogs are allowed, please keep them on leads as parts of the route go through areas with livestock.

Terrain: Follows the coastal footpath, with a downhill section to the bay, so you may want to take it easy on the way back up. A walk through a wooded valley, including muddy woodland floors and an uneven stony path. The walk starts with a steep descent into the valley and ends by climbing back up the same hill. The beach at the halfway point has a pebble ridge.

🏴 Mae disgrifiad Cymraeg o'r daith hon ar ein gwefan

Starting point: Southgate car park

1. From the car park, bear right and follow the path as it winds its way along the coastal slope. Look out for the limestone soil-loving flowers such as thrift and spring squill, that make a wonderful display in spring.

2. Continue along the coast as you leave the houses of West Cliff behind you, until you gradually begin to go downhill.

3. You will gradually descend into the sand area of the dunes of Three Cliffs Bay. Lizards often bask on the hot sand here during summer; look out for them scampering away as you approach.

4. Continue down until you reach the bottom, the perfect place to enjoy a picnic. If you fancy a further stroll then continue to the river and cross the stepping stones. Here, along the river valley, you'll find a fantastic view of the ruins of Pennard Castle.

Top Three Cliffs Bay in the evening

Right The ruins of Pennard Castle

26 TOURING THE COAST

N
200 m
Pennard Burrows
Southgate
Southgate Farm
Pennard Pill
Pobbles Beach
Shire Combe
West Cliff
Fox Hole
Three Cliffs Bay
1
2
3
4
P

Nicholaston Burrows and Oxwich Bay
Perlau arfordirol

With its dunes, sandy beach and clifftop path, this stretch of coastline is the perfect destination for a day by the sea, preferably with a picnic and a swimsuit.

Sat between the high ridge of Cefn Bryn, which runs through the centre of Gower, and the sea, this strip of land is a tapestry of different habitats. A ribbon of woodland yields to dunes and sand. Sandstone cliffs with rocky promontories (Little Tor and Great Tor) are backed by open heathland.

The beach stretches as far as Nicolaston Pill, a stream that drains the marshes behind the dunes and divides the beach, which is privately owned by the Penrice estate. In 1967, the National Trust acquired the shoreline beyond the stream to Three Cliffs Bay and its hinterland.

The walk to Nicholaston Burrows from the car park at Oxwich Bay takes 15–20 minutes, either along the sandy beach or through the dunes that fringe it (see page 30). It moves you away from the more popular end of the beach to a quieter, less visited stretch – well worth it if you have the time.

Above Oxwich Pill soon after a January sunrise. The pill drains to Oxwich Marsh. Nicholaston Woods is on the right

Right Bloody cranesbill, which grows at Nicholaston Burrows

yswydden twyni tywod **coed** gwenyn **corsdir**
tegeirian bera madfall **rhosyn bwrned**

Wildflowers in the dunes

Nicholaston Burrows' dunes provide an ideal habitat for a variety of plants, some very rare, which burst into bloom in the summer. Bloody cranesbill, burnet rose, pyramidal orchid and wild privet all flourish here. The Trust cuts back any trees that have seeded here from the nearby woods, as they smother the delicate wildflowers. The dunes are also covered with multi-coloured, fascinating lichen. Look out for both as you walk through the Burrows.

This is also an important biological site: there are five Red Data List and 28 nationally scarce invertebrates here, including sharp-tailed bees, pied-wing robberflies and the *Dicronychus equisetiodes* beetle.

Oxwich Bay

Nicholaston Burrows overlooks Oxwich Bay National Nature Reserve (not National Trust), a generous, two-and-a-half mile (four-kilometre) arc of sandy beach which is popular during the summer months. It is easily accessible from a car park, making it attractive to sailors and water skiers. A footpath from the beach takes visitors through the extensive dune system along the cliffs, around Oxwich Point and on to Port Eynon Bay.

Above Oxwich Bay at sunrise in January, taken from Little Tor. Nicholaston Burrows are to the right and Oxwich Point is in the distance

✓ THINGS TO DO AT NICHOLASTON BURROWS

Explore the dunes
How many wildflowers can you spot? You might even see a lizard.

Paddle
The gentle slope of the beach in Oxwich Bay is the perfect place to jump over the waves as they roll in.

Put up a windbreak, build a sandcastle, sunbathe
The sandy beach is a popular spot for traditional seaside activities during the summer.

Swim
This is one of the safest beaches on Gower.

WALK THIS WAY
Nicholaston Bay circular walk
O gopa craig i gefn bryn

Explore clifftop paths and moorland. If the tide is out, you can also take in a detour to the beach.

- Moderate
- 2 hours
- 4.5 miles/7.2km
- Dog friendly

Please note: Although dogs are welcome on this walk, livestock is present at points on the route

Terrain: varied, metalled roads, heathland, clifftop paths, stony tracks. Some steep sections but no stiles.

 Mae disgrifiad Cymraeg o'r daith hon ar ein gwefan

Start: Penmaen bus stop or National Trust car park.

1. From the bus stop, walk up the lane to the right of the church. After the cattle grid, fork right onto a track past the National Trust cairn and through the car park. Follow the track past Myrtle Cottage, keep left and, at a gateway, turn left and continue with a stone wall on your right. Just past the end of the wall, bear right under the telegraph wires. When the path meets a stony track, turn left. At Gower Way stone marker, turn right going straight uphill on to the moor known as Cefn Bryn.

2. At the top of the hill you will pass a fenced mound which is a reservoir. Walk 550 yards (0.5km) further, then turn sharp left on to the stony grass track just before the Gower Way marker, before the path starts to go uphill.

3. At the lane, turn left. Cross over the main road on to a lane. After a gate with a Welsh Water sign, turn left down the steps. After a short while there will be another set of steps on right. Keep to the left and follow the clifftop path.

Alternative route if tide is out
Go right, down the steps and continue straight on through dune slacks and over the dunes on to the beach. Turn left.
   Continue around the cliff outcrop called Little Tor, then head back to the back of Tor Bay to find the path winding up on to the clifftop. At the top, a path comes in from left. Bear to right in front of bench. Now go to *, point 5.)

Top The sea creeps onto the beach at Tor Bay

Left A pony on Cefn Bryn

30 TOURING THE COAST

4. Keep to the left through a sandy patch and continue on the clifftop path. You will eventually pass a restored lime kiln on the right.

5. After the lime kiln, the path forks. Keep right shortly after a bridlepath comes in from the right. This is where walkers from the beach rejoin the route. Continue straight on along the narrow path. * At a wider grassy path, bear right. Follow the path around the headland of Great Tor.

6. After passing the ringwork, follow the path as it bears around to the left.

7. Go through a gate on to a concrete path. Turn right at the main road and take the first left on to a lane. Follow this lane to take you back to the car park and the bus stop at the start of the walk.

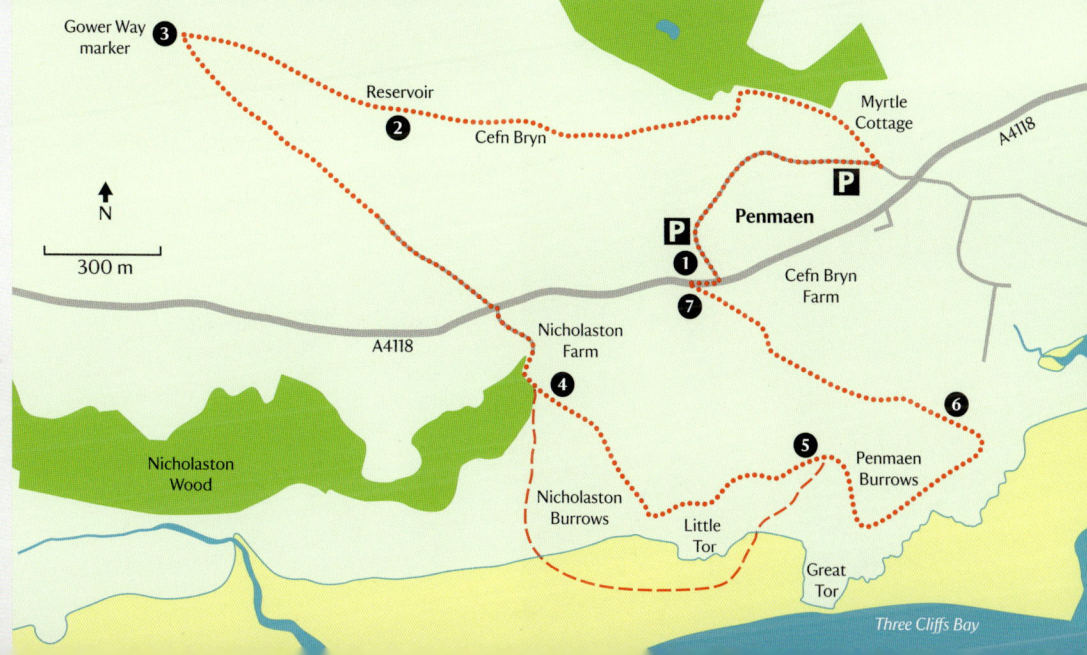

The South Coast
Arfordir y De

The ragged coastline of South Gower has been formed over the centuries by the sea battering and infiltrating the limestone, dissolving it into a series of caves, coves and headlands.

Prehistoric man, seabirds, smugglers and rock climbers have all, one way or another, made use of these interesting formations. Today's visitors enjoy activities from fossil hunting to rock pooling.

Looking after the coast

The National Trust owns most of this shoreline, which stretches from Fall Bay to Port Eynon Point (find out more about the different areas on page 34). We manage it with the help of The Wildlife Trust for South and West Wales. This means this wild and remote place is safe from property developers and commercial activities, keeping its natural beauty, far-reaching views and abundant wildlife safe for the future.

⊙ LOOK OUT FOR

Birds
South Gower's cliffs provide nesting sites for kittiwakes, although these can only be seen from the sea. Clifftop grassland is inhabited by linnets, meadow pipits, stonechats and Dartford warblers, all attracted by its gorse and scrub habitat. Oystercatchers peck for food along the shore.

Butterflies
Grayling butterflies abound on the limestone crags during August.

Insects
Bloody-nosed beetles can readily be seen on the coast path in the summer months. Green tiger beetles like sandy areas among vegetation and can be sighted at Overton Mere, both in the Wildlife Trust reserve and the bay looked after by the National Trust.

Lichens
The cliff faces are encrusted with different species of this interesting plant, including scrambled-egg lichen, which is a threatened species in the UK.

Moths
Silky wave moths can be seen at Overton Mere.

Wildflowers
The limestone grassland has many varieties of flowering plants including common rock rose, eyebright, milkwort, spring squill, thyme and tree mallow.

Above Fall Bay in late afternoon in January. Thurba Head and the Knave can be seen in the distance

Left The funnel-shaped flower of a tree mallow tends to come out in summer; the shrub is medium-sized and semi-evergreen

Talcenni craig ac ogofâu yn herio'r gwynt a'r tonnau

✓ THINGS TO DO ON THE SOUTH COAST

Catch a fish for supper
Anglers cast off from Tears Point, near Fall Bay, in the hope of hooking bass, cod, flounder, mackerel, mullet, pollack and whiting.

Climb a rock
61-metre (200-foot) high Thurba Head is popular with climbers. Not for the inexperienced!

Explore the rockpools
The rocky shoreline is peppered with these miniature worlds, which are exposed at low tide.

Go for a paddle
Refresh your feet after walking down to a beach.

Go fossil hunting
The limestone cliffs are made up of the compressed remains of sea creatures, squashed very small. Look closely and you may see fossilised shells and coral poking out of the rock.

Left The robin-sized stonechat has a sharp, loud call that sounds like two stones being tapped together

TOURING THE COAST 33

Areas of South Gower
Camu drwy haenau o hanes

The sheer cliffs, caves and sandy coves here are less accessible than other parts of Gower but well worth the walk to reach them.

Fall Bay

Although Fall Bay is close to Rhossili, it is less accessible and therefore blissfully uncrowded. The path from Rhossili village hall takes you across fields and stiles and then down a steep and sometimes slippery descent to the beach.

Thurba Bay

Thurba Head, a 61-metre (200-foot) jagged high headland that towers over Mewslade Bay, was given to the National Trust in 1933. The bay is reached by walking along a woody path, then through a valley. Much less visited than Rhossili, although popular with surfers, it has a sandy beach and plenty of rockpools, both of which are revealed at low tide. Exposed limestone strata (layers of sedimentary rock whose unusual internal characteristics distinguish it from other layers) are clearly visible in vertical bands striping the sheer cliff faces and on the incisor-shaped Knave which protrudes jaggedly from the sea.

Port Eynon

The sweep of beach at Port Eynon Bay is a minute away from the car park and a popular spot in the summer. Port Eynon once bustled with fishermen unloading lobster pots from smacks, boats transporting limestone to Devon, and excise men on the trail of smugglers. These days, it still bustles but with visitors enjoying the pretty village of whitewashed cottages and its tea rooms and curl of beach.

Above Sunlight on the rocks at Thurba Head, looking east

Right A family plays on Port Eynon beach

cimwch bythynnod **mamoth** pyllau llanw sgerbwd fflint **caffi**
breichled ifori nodwyddau asgwrn ogof Paviland
dannedd ceirw smyglwyr

The mystery of Paviland Cave

Cut into Paviland's limestone cliffs, the caves along Gower's south coast once provided places of shelter and storage for the peninsula's early inhabitants. Evidence of these early cave dwellers was unearthed in January 1823, when geologist Professor William Buckland found the remains of a mammoth and headless skeleton in a cave – now known as Goat's Hole – below Paviland Farm. The skeleton was stained with red ochre and became known as the Red Lady of Paviland. Buckland dated it from Roman times but in the 1890s he was proved incorrect when another archaeologist found flint tools possibly made by Stone Age man 70,000 years previously. In 1912, Professor William Sollas made a further excavation and study of the skeleton. He revealed that the skeleton was in fact a young man who lived 30,000 years ago. Other finds included reindeer teeth bored for necklaces, mammoth-ivory bracelets and bone needles and worked flints, all of which give us an indication of how prehistoric man lived and died.

Goat's Hole today

Now recognisable from its pear-shaped entrance, Goat's Hole is one of the larger Paviland Caves and would have been formed by the sea, when water levels were significantly higher than today. When daylight gleams through the cave's 'chimney' just right, you can see hollows on the cave floor – remnants of the two 19th-century excavations. However it's best to just imagine how this looks, as it's not usually safe to visit the cave in person.

Below The entrance to Paviland Cave, as seen from the sea

'The Bristol Channel swashing against the jagged rock beneath the cave, Lundy Island in the distance, the coast of south-west England beyond that.'

Stephen Moss describes the view from Goat's Hole cave in the *Guardian*, 2011

TOURING THE COAST 35

Culver Hole
Cyfrinach o'r Oesoedd Canol

Mae'r grisiau a'r blychau craig y tu ôl i'r wal drwchus, ynghyd â'r ffenestri bob siâp, yn awgrymu mai colomendy oedd hwn – nid cuddfan i smyglwyr. Enw o'r Hen Saesneg am golomen yw 'Culver' Roedd yr adar yn cyflenwi cig ac wyau drwy'r flwyddyn.

Set into a cliff face, this mysterious medieval construction baffles visitors and experts alike. There are rumours it was used by smugglers, that a secret tunnel once linked it to a salthouse at Port Eynon and that carrier pigeons used to send messages were housed here, but nothing can be substantiated.

Only accessible at low tide or by a perilous scramble from a clifftop path above it (which we don't recommend), Culver Hole is one of Gower's most remote and curious places. Originally a tall, narrow sea cave between two stone cliff faces, it was bricked up with masonry two-metres (six-and-a-half foot) thick during the Middle Ages, most probably during the 13th and 14th centuries.

What was it for?

Behind the 18-metre (60-foot) brick wall, which is pierced with windows of various shapes and sizes, lie 30 tiers of small compartments and a flight of steps. Much speculation surrounds the purpose of this construction. Some say it was intended as a smuggler's hide-out, others say a sort of residence, or a depot for a nearby (now demolished) manor house, but most agree that one of its most likely uses was as a pigeon house. The clue lies in the word 'culver', which derives from the Old English for pigeon or dove. During Medieval times, before they headed inland to the rich pickings available in towns, pigeons were common on the coast, especially the Coastal Blue Rock Pigeon. Given shelter and food, they bred all year round and provided essential meat and eggs during winter months when not much else was available. Many purpose-built pigeon and dove cotes were constructed as a result.

Left The window slits as seen from the outside of Culver Hole

Rhossili Down
Ar gefnen gul Rhos Sulien

Walk to the summit of Rhossili Down and, on a clear day, you will be rewarded with a mind-clearing vista of the entire Gower Peninsula. At 193 metres (632 feet) above sea level, this is the highest point on Gower and offers 360 degree views across Rhossili Bay to West Wales and North Devon.

It's also the largest of all Gower's commons at 345 hectares (875 acres).

The National Trust acquired Rhossili Down – which is designated an SSSI and Special Area of Conservation – in 1967. Its aim was to protect this important coastal landscape from development and to conserve its wildlife heritage. Unlike most of the peninsula with its free-draining limestone, Rhossili Down is a massive lump of Old Red Sandstone covered with bracken and heather, with acid, boggy ground on its lower slopes. Both habitats are important for a variety of plant, insect, animal and bird species (see page 40).

Part of the Trust's management of the land involves grazing animals. Sheep and ponies – many owned by local people – nibble tree seedlings and scrub, preventing them from swamping more vulnerable plants. Banks, hedges and dry stone walls must also be looked after to provide shelter for crops and animals against the fierce sea wind. The result is a species-rich habitat that pops with colour and hops with life all year round.

Rhossili's history

As you walk over Rhossili Down, look out for unusual rocks and stones emerging from the gorse and heather. These are signs of habitation by prehistoric people, notably places they would have buried or honoured their dead.

The most noticeable is Sweynes Howes. However, although it's named after a Viking chief, it is unlikely it actually had anything to do with the Vikings. This pair of Neolithic burial tombs lies on the eastern slope of the Down and was built between 4,000 and 5,000 years ago, as were the five cairns (burial monuments) on the north side of the summit.

North of Rhossili Down, on Llanmadoc Hill, is The Bulwark, an Iron Age hill fort. This was a large, defended enclosure and its banks and ditches are well preserved and easy to spot.

Evidence of more recent history is the remains of the radar station at the north western end of Rhossili Down. During the Second World War, this sent early warning signals of approaching enemy planes to Swansea.

rhedyn cloddiau beddrodau merlod Oes Haearn defaid gorsaf radar Oes y Cerrig tywodfaen coch grug tir comin caer Ail Ryfel Byd llafn y bladur Oes Efydd

Right The prehistoric Sweynes Howes stone atop Rhossili Down

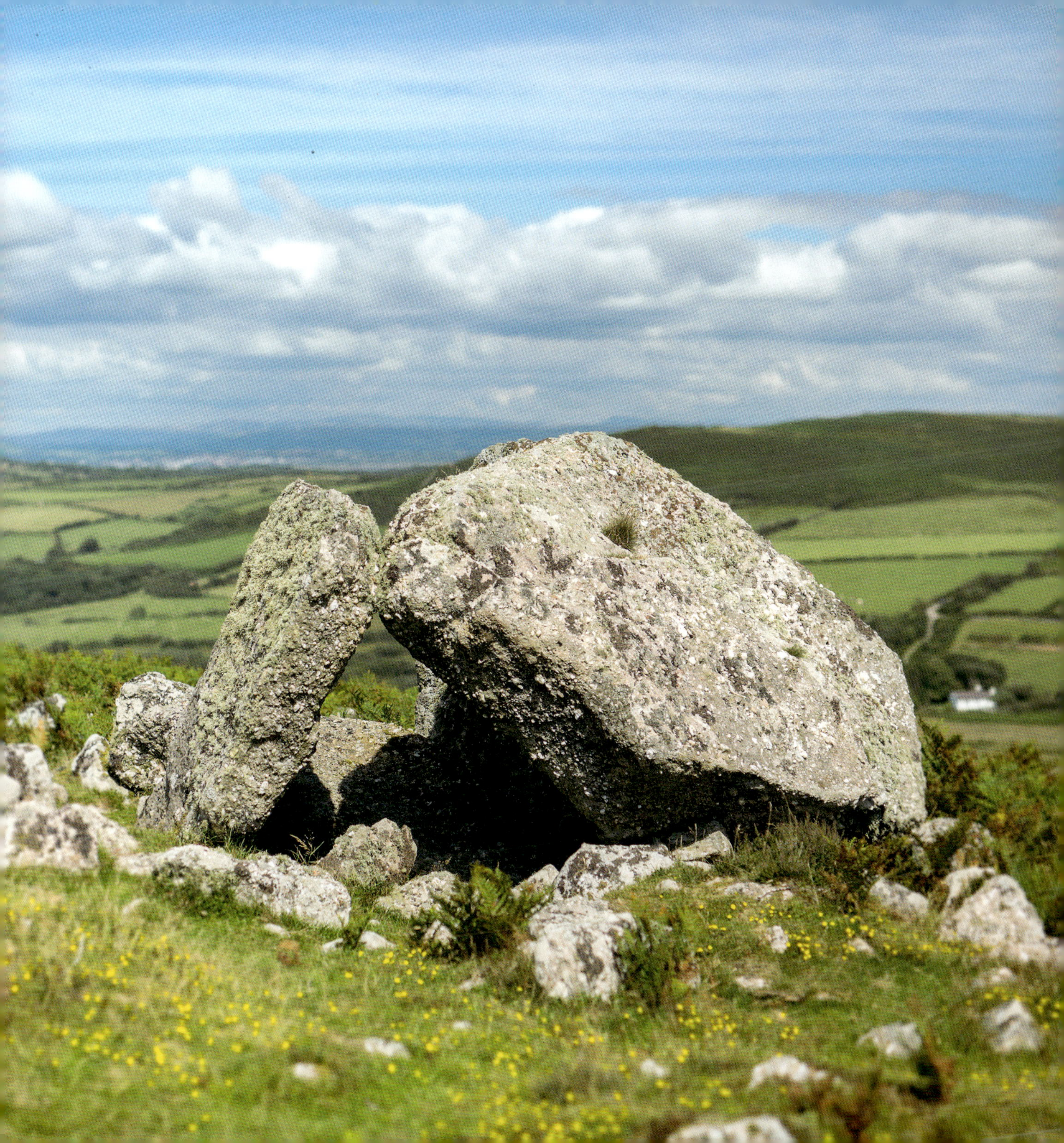

Highlights of Rhossili Down
Profiadau bythgofiadwy

Whether you're looking for adrenalin-fuelled adventure or prefer to sit back and enjoy nature, Rhossili Down has something for everyone.

⊙ LOOK OUT FOR

Heathland plants
Bell heather, ling heather, tormentil and western gorse all thrive here and cover the ground with a patchwork of yellow and purple flowers in spring and summer.

Rare insects
Southern damselflies and black bog ants have become endangered due to the destruction of heathland nationally, but thrive on Rhossili Down.

The brown hare
Larger than rabbits with longer legs and ears, brown hares are most visible during their breeding season in the spring.

Above Rhossili is an unbeatable spot to watch the sun set

Far left A male southern damselfly rests on a blade of grass

Left Brown hares often bound in a zigzag pattern, powered by their powerful legs

✓ THINGS TO DO ON RHOSSILI DOWN

Go geocaching
The National Trust organises digital treasure hunts on Rhossili Down. Pick up a GPS unit from the National Trust Shop and Visitor Centre in Rhossili village and set off.

Stay at The Old Rectory
This former home of the rector of Rhossili and Llangennith is now owned by the National Trust and let for holidays. Situated in a romantic and remote spot – it is the only building above Rhossili Bay – it has enormous views of the sea and Worms Head. Allegedly Dylan Thomas once considered living here, but changed his mind on discovering Rhossili village didn't have a pub. *For information, nationaltrustholidays.org.uk*

Volunteer
The Trust welcomes volunteers to help with its conservation work on Gower, including maintenance of dry stone walls, beach cleans and habitat management. This could be for one day, a working holiday or a longer-term arrangement. *For information on volunteering on Gower, call 01792 390636. For information on working holidays, nationaltrust.org.uk/working-holidays.*

Watch the sunset
There's no place better to see the sun sink into the horizon than from the top of Rhossili Down. Bring a blanket and Thermos.

Left You can try geocaching on Rhossili Down

sgwarnog grug **golygfa** eithin **tresgl y moch** awyr iach **morgrug** Pen y pyrod **geogelcio** machlud **mursennod** hedfan

Rhossili Bay
Milltiroedd o draeth hudolus

The three-mile sandy stretch of beach at Rhossili Bay is Gower's most famous, and most visited, place.

It's not surprising that it features on countless 'Best Beaches' lists, in television programmes and appeared in the opening ceremony of the 2012 Olympics – it's breathtaking, photogenic and never fails to impress and inspire. The firm sand scoured by the pounding of waves from the Atlantic is an exhilarating destination for walkers, runners and riders, and the wind-whipped sea with its crest-after-crest of crashing waves makes for ideal surfing conditions.

The beach is book-ended by two tidal islands: Worms Head (see page 46) at the southern end, and the smaller Burry Holms at the northern. Accessible at low tide, Burry Holms is the location of several early settlements: the remains of a medieval hermit's cell and an early fortified camp can still be seen.

A lost village: The Warren

Rhossili Village sits on the clifftop overlooking the bay, but an early settlement – dating from the 12th and 13th centuries – was once situated on a perilous strip of land close to the beach. Today nothing can be seen of this village, known as The Warren, but it once had its own church and graveyard (human bones have surfaced from time to time) which was discovered during excavation by archaeologists in 1979–80. It is thought that severe storms in the 14th century buried The Warren in sand, a fate suffered by other villages along the South Wales coast.

Wrecked remains

Walk along the beach at Rhossili towards Worms Head when the tide is low and you will come across the skeletal ribs of a ship's bow poking from the sand. This is *The Helvetia*, a sailing ship wrecked off Worms Head in the 19th century (see page 7). Gower's rocky coastline has always been a dangerous place for ships. Often shrouded by mist or heavy rain and subjected to ferocious winds, it has seen many ships smashed on the rocks by Atlantic storms.

LOOK OUT FOR

Grey seals
They have been seen in the water off Worms Head (see page 46).

Seabirds
Cormorants, fulmars, oystercatchers and sanderlings are often sighted on the Worms Head causeway.

Shellfish
Limpets and barnacles can be spotted on the beach.

You won't find
Any specimen trees. The constant salt-laden winds from the Atlantic prevent any apart from the odd wind-bent hawthorn from growing.

THINGS TO DO AT RHOSSILI BAY

Buy a book or a postcard
The former Coastguard Cottages in Rhossili village are now the National Trust shop and Visitor Centre.

Fly a kite or go kite surfing
Winds whipping in off the sea provide perfect currents for these airborne activities.

Go rockpooling
Look for anemones, brittle stars, sea urchins, crabs, limpets and prawns in the pools lining the bay.

Go surfing
The Atlantic rollers crashing onto Rhossili beach are popular with surfers, who head to the beach at Llangennith in their campervans during the summer.

tywod meudwy pentre' coll mulfran
pyllau llanw *The Helvetia* syrffio
hedfan barcud morloi llongddrylliad
mynwent pibydd y tywod

Left The pathway to Rhossili beach

Right A surfer on Rhossili

WALK THIS WAY

Rhossili Down, Hillend and Rhossili beach
Copa gwych a golygfa braf

This challenging walk takes you to the highest point on Gower, through ancient landscapes and past burial chambers, radar stations and shipwrecks, before finishing at one of Britain's best beaches.

- Challenging
- 2 hours 30 mins
- 5 miles/8km
- Dog friendly, providing they are kept under control – livestock is present on this route throughout the year.

Terrain: this walk covers a variety of terrain including steep footpaths, uneven tracks, a sandy beach and steep steps to the finish.

Mae disgrifiad Cymraeg o'r daith hon ar ein gwefan

Start: National Trust shop, Rhossili

1. At the bus stop, follow the footpath as it bears left towards the churchyard and past St Mary's Church, which was built in the 12th–13th century. Look out for the unmarked sailor's grave in the corner of the churchyard. At the junction with the stony track, go left and continue until you reach the gate marked with a National Trust sign for Rhossili Down.

2. Head up the hill through the heathland. If you look back towards Rhossili village you will see the medieval strip field system of The Vile on the headland (see page 50).

3. Continue on the main path along the ridge of the Down. The beacon marks the highest point on Gower and is also the site of a Bronze-Age cairn built around 4,000 years ago. As you continue along the ridge path, you will pass the remains of Stone Age burial chambers, Sweynes Howes.

4. The vegetation on the ridge path is predominantly heathland and presents a dazzling display of pinks and purples in late summer. Further down the slope to the right there are areas of wet heath. The plants here, such as bog asphodel and cross-leaved heath, are visible but care should be taken if exploring as it can be extremely boggy at times.

5. As you approach half way along the Down you will see the remains of a Second World War radar

Above The view north, to Rhossili beach, from Rhossili Down. The beacon marks the highest point on the Gower

Left The late Norman St Mary's Church; its archway – with dogtooth and chevron mouldings – is locally celebrated

station in front of you. Continue through here and up the slope on the far side. The radar station was built to provide early warning of threats to Swansea from German bomber planes.

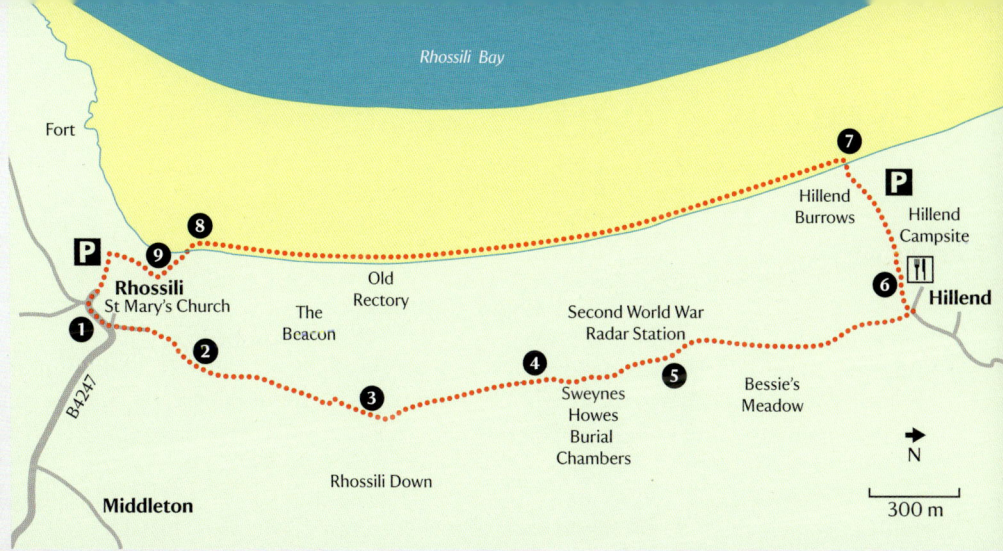

6. From here the path descends steeply towards Hillend campsite. Go into the site and straight on past Eddie's Café and turn left on to the beach. You are approximately half way around now and this may be the perfect opportunity for a cup of tea and to rest your feet.

7. Turn left onto the beach and head back towards Rhossili. The muddy cliff to your left is actually the remains of a glacial feature known as a solifluction terrace. Soil would slip from Rhossili Down whenever the ice melted a little and over time built up into the raised area we see today. Look out for the remains of *The Helvetia*, which was shipwrecked on the beach in 1887.

8. Once you have passed *The Helvetia*, look for the bottom of the steps on your left, as they mark the route back to Rhossili Village. Admire the views over the beach and across to Carmarthen and south Pembrokeshire.

9. At the top, turn right to head towards the car park and National Trust shop, or enjoy a meal or snack in one of several cafés and tea shops in the village.

Above A signpost marks the route

TOURING THE COAST 45

Worms Head
Pen y Pyrod

It is easy to see how Worms Head got its name. 'Wurm' is Old Norse for dragon or serpent, which is what invading Vikings thought it resembled.

With its sinuous shape and humped, rocky spine, the headland does indeed appear to slither into the ocean from the southern end of Rhossili Bay, especially at high tide when all that is visible are its 'head' and 'coils'. Seen through a sea mist on a winter morning, it appears to rise like a creature from a primordial swamp, which may account for the many myths and magical notions attributed to it.

The perilous tide

Worms Head is a mile-long tidal island – it can only be reached for about two-and-a-half hours a day at low tide via a rocky causeway. Many walkers have misjudged the timing and either attempted the crossing and been swept away by the sea, or found themselves stranded. One of these was a young Dylan Thomas who fell asleep and got marooned. 'I stayed on that Worm,' the poet recalled, 'from dusk to midnight, sitting on that top grass, frightened to go farther in because of the rats and because of things I am ashamed to be frightened of. Then the tips of the reef began to poke out of the water and, perilously, I climbed along them to the shore.'

Areas to discover

Don't let that put you off, however; judge the tide times right and Worms Head is well worth exploring. A National Nature Reserve that is owned and protected by the National Trust, it remains unspoiled and wild.

The land mass nearest the mainland is Inner Head, which has a large variety of wild flowers including scurvy grass, sea campion and thrift. Outer Head is reached by walking along Low Neck, then crossing Devil's Bridge, a natural limestone arch caused by the sea powering through the rock. Outer Head is rockier terrain with 60-metre (197-foot) high, jagged cliff faces – perfect nesting places for seabirds – and a natural blow hole which emits noisy booms and hisses when waves pound into it.

Farming on Worms Head

Despite its inaccessibility, Worms Head's fertile land – particularly at Inner Head – has been farmed for centuries, principally by sheep farmers making the most of the rich grazing. It has been said sheep who have a taste of the lush turf here don't want to eat anywhere else afterwards.

Once, a man grew a crop of potatoes on the south side of the island; he was successful but the endeavour was eventually stymied by the logistics of getting them back to the mainland to sell.

Right A view of Worms Head from Rhossili Down at sunset

Y bore bach a'i niwl sy'n dod â hud i Ben y Pyrod

✓ THINGS TO DO ON WORMS HEAD

Bring a camera
There are plenty of photo opportunities on Worms Head, from wheeling birds to pounding waves and views of Rhossili Bay.

Go fishing
Sea bass can be caught from boats during the summer.

Keep an eye on the tide
Make sure you don't get stranded!

Pack a picnic
There are no cafés on Worms Head, so don't forget your sandwiches.

◉ LOOK OUT FOR

Birds
The cliffs of Outer Head are nesting and feeding sites for black-back gulls, guillemots, herring gulls and kittiwakes, among others.

Grey seals
These are often seen in the bays and around the coast of Rhossili.

Jellyfish
Including Velella (by-the-wind sailor), these live on the surface of the ocean.

> 'The old worm's blowing, time for a boat to be going.'
>
> Old Gower saying, deriving from the booming noise made by the blowhole

TOURING THE COAST 47

WALK THIS WAY
Serpents, seascapes and shipwrecks
Herio'r sarff

This walk takes in views of one of Wales' best beaches, medieval farming systems and the mythical Worms Head.

- Easy
- 30 minutes
- 1 mile/1.6km
- Dog friendly – but please be aware that livestock (usually sheep) graze here for most of the year.

Terrain: Accessible to all. The walk is on a gentle gradient sloping downhill from the start and uphill on the return leg. The coast path here is a disabled access track and therefore level and even. The final 110yds (100m) or so to the coastguard lookout is on very short/flat grass and uphill. No stiles to cross, one gate at the start.

🏴 Mae disgrifiad Cymraeg o'r daith hon ar ein gwefan

Start: National Trust Shop, Rhossili

1. With your back to the bus stop, turn right and walk along the road, continuing between the car park and the Worms Head Hotel. The National Trust shop is a little further on your left.

2. The National Trust shop is in one of the former coastguard cottages. The powerful tides and shifting sands caused many shipwrecks. The remains of the *The Helvetia* can still be seen on Rhossili beach at low tide.

3. Continue to follow the path through the gateway on the surfaced path.

4. To the right of the path there are a series of mounds. These are the remains of an Iron Age fort. The magnificent views from here meant the inhabitants of the fort could see their enemies for miles around.

5. As you continue along the surfaced track you will see fields and hedge banks which are part of a medieval open field strip system. The Normans introduced this system of farming in the 12th century.

6. Where the surfaced track bears sharp left, walk straight on following a wide grass path towards the coastguard lookout where you will have a spectacular view of Worms Head.

7. The coastguard lookout was built in Victorian times and is now manned by volunteers.

8. Once you have reached the Coastguard lookout, you can make the choice to cross onto the island or return to the start by the route you've travelled.

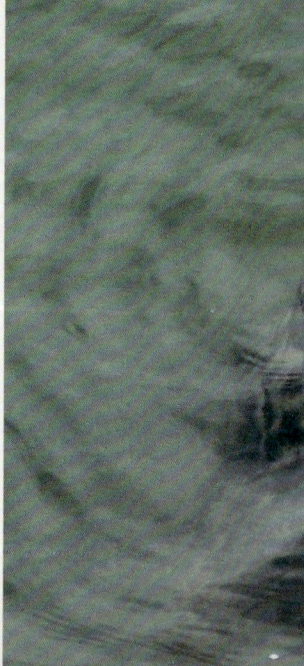

Top The view over Rhossili Down to Worms Head
Right A seal spotted in the waters near Worms Head

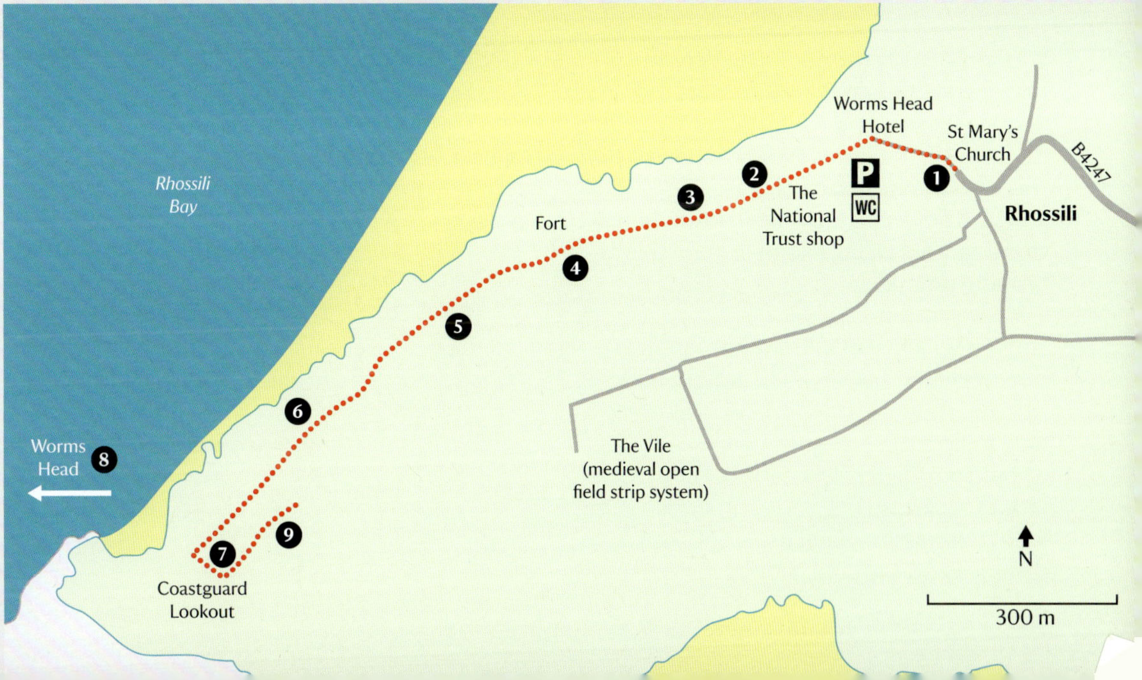
Rhossili Bay
Worms Head Hotel
St Mary's Church
B4247
Rhossili
The National Trust shop
Fort
The Vile (medieval open field strip system)
Worms Head
Coastguard Lookout
1
2
3
4
5
6
7
8
9
N
300 m

The Vile
Caeau brith o'r Canol Oesoedd

You could easily overlook The Vile, an unremarkable-looking 158-hectare (391-acre) field system beyond the National Trust shop at Rhossili. It's not immediately apparent that this unassuming patch of grass, stone walls and wild flowers is an important historical site: a rare surviving example of medieval farming practices.

Look closer and you will see banks of earth about three feet (one metre) wide – called landshares – between narrow strips of land. These strips were individually owned by different villagers who shared this fertile, frost-free field. Each farmer could own one or several strips, as long as each strip was in a different part of The Vile so that the good and poor soil was shared equally.

These narrow strips were a common feature of medieval field systems, especially in South Wales.

Crops ranged from cereals – barley, oats and wheat – to vegetables such as mangolds, swede and potatoes, some of which were sold in the markets at Swansea and Cardiff. These crops were rotated, with some strips left fallow after cropping to reduce pests and allow the soil to regain fertility.

The Vile was subject to common rights, which meant that after harvest, everyone had the right to graze stock there until St Andrew's Day, 30 November. This cleared the site of the remains of the crop and provided manure for next year's.

Above An aerial view of the Vile's medieval field system

Right A male linnet perches on flowering gorse

cloddiau **nico** melyn yr ŷd **tatws** llinos **pabi** maip trilliw bach **bras melyn** ceirch **aredig** ehedydd **waliau**

A brief history of farming on The Vile

The Vile dates from Norman times and possibly earlier – its name is the Old Gower pronunciation for 'field'. But its earliest records are from the 18th century. In 1780, the strip holders consisted of six farmers from Rhossili and seven from neighbouring Middleton, with the size of holdings ranging from under an acre to 20 hectares (49 acres).

Strip farming continued until the 19th century, when most Rhossili villagers had a strip on The Vile. Many of the original strips have since been amalgamated, creating larger fields, but many originals also remain. This is largely due to the remoteness of Rhossili and the constancy of farming practice and ownership here. Little changed on the peninsula for centuries – something we are grateful for today.

Looking after The Vile

As agriculture and agricultural machinery have become more efficient and fields have grown larger, most of Britain's strip systems have disappeared. Because Gower is remote and was largely unvisited, The Vile has survived, and it's important we continue to preserve such a rare example of medieval open-field cultivation.

To ensure The Vile remains looked after, the National Trust purchased 57 hectares (141 acres) of land within it. The Trust maintains and restores the banks, protecting the field boundaries. Crops are planted to encourage arable wild flowers once common here, such as corn marigold, lesser weasel snout and poppies, to flourish once more. The Vile is like a giant bird table: two fields are planted sparsely with barley to allow rare arable wild flowers to grow during the summer and then the crop is left unharvested to provide food for farmland birds during winter.

Above A small tortoiseshell butterfly rests open-winged on buddleia

How to get there

The Vile is on the south-western tip of Gower, before Worms Head. Reach it by walking along the cliff from the National Trust shop toward Rhossili Point. The Vile is on your left, over the stone wall. The best view of it is from the top of Rhossili Down.

⊙ LOOK OUT FOR

Birds
Chaffinches, goldfinches, linnets, skylarks, starlings, wrens and yellowhammers.

Butterflies
Common blues and small tortoiseshells.

TOURING THE COAST 51

Whiteford Burrows

Traeth mwyaf gogleddol Gŵyr

Even in the summer there are days when visitors to Whiteford Burrows find they have its three-mile beach to themselves. But although this miniature peninsula, the most northern point of the Gower, is less accessible than Rhossili (it is reached by a short walk from a car park), it is no less interesting.

An NNR, SSSI and Special Area of Conservation, Whiteford Burrows has a variety of habitats. On the west is Whiteford Sands, a long, sandy stretch of beach backed by dunes and pine forest; the dynamic sand dune system is ranked among the best dune sites in Wales. On the east lie the mud flats of Llanrhidian Marsh (see page 60) and to the south, the newly-created saltmarsh of Cwm Ivy (see page 54). Each habitat attracts its own range of wildlife, from wading birds, wildfowl and insects to rare and unusual plants, such as dune gentian, fen orchid and petalwort.

Whiteford Burrows is an important site for the National Trust. Acquired in 1965, it was the first land to be purchased with funds from the Trust's coastal campaign, Enterprise Neptune. The Trust saved it from becoming a landfill site, and what could have been wasteland is now an important conservation area.

LOOK OUT FOR

Birds
Lapwings, little ringed plovers, ospreys, skylarks, tree creepers.

Insects
Common blue and marbled white butterflies, glow worms, great green bush crickets.

Plants
Bee orchid, bloody cranesbill, cowslip, dune gentian, marsh iris.

Above A view of Whiteford Burrows and Sands

Bottom left Bee orchids get their name from their main pollinator – though in the UK they are self-pollinated

Bottom centre The striking and distinctive marbled white butterfly

Bottom right Secluded Burrows Cottage, now a holiday home

---

tegeirian y fign   coedwig   crëyr bach   Gwarchodfa Natur Genedlaethol   briallu Mair   crwynllys Cymreig   twyni tywod   gweirlöyn cleisiog   cornchwiglen   pry' tân   cwtiad torchog bach   tegeirian y wenynen   gwalch y pysgod

✓ THINGS TO DO AT WHITEFORD BURROWS

Bird watch
Egrets and ospreys have been sighted in the area. Pick a spot at one of the hides at Cwm Ivy or on Berges Island at the tip of Whiteford Burrows, which was a tidal island but is now part of the mainland.

Fly a kite on Whiteford Sands
Watch the wind whip it into the air.

Look for fen orchid and gold lichen
These plants have established themselves in the dunes.

Stay at Burrows Cottage
This former forester's house in the pine woods is a short walk from the dunes. *For more information, nationaltrustholidays.org.uk.*

Around Whiteford Burrows
Crwydro ardal Whiteford

Llanmadoc Hill, Ryers Down and Cheriton
This 78-hectare (193-acre) common near Cwm Ivy and Whiteford Burrows is dominated by bracken, grasses, gorse and heather which create a rich mixture of yellow and pink in late summer. Patches of marshy grassland bristle with tussocks of purple moor grass which provide shelter for the marsh fritillary butterflies.

Cwm Ivy: a new saltmarsh
Visit the saltmarsh at Cwm Ivy and you will witness a rapidly changing landscape. For centuries, this was farmland, created by the construction of a sea defence in the Middle Ages, built to keep the ocean at bay. But in August 2014, this was breached by a storm.

Rather than rebuild the wall and defy the sea, the National Trust allowed the natural process of the sea coming in to continue. The changes have been remarkable. Farmland grasses have died back, trees have lost their leaves and become standing wood (appreciated by insects and woodpeckers) and saltmarsh plants such as English scurvy grass and sea blight have taken hold. It's also an important site for wetland flies, including rare soldier flies. The result is a wildlife-rich saltmarsh that gets richer by the day.

Right The view south from Ryers Down

Mae llethrau bryn Llanmadog yn gymysg o borffor ac aur yn yr haf ac yn gynefin i löyn byw brith y gors. Islaw mae newidiadau syfrdanol yng Nghwm Ivy, ers i forglawdd canol oesol gael ei chwalu gan storm yn 2014. Mae morfa heli yn datblygu o'r newydd dan ddylanwad y llanw, a bywyd gwyllt ar gynnydd. Yng ngheg yr aber y mae'r enghraifft olaf o oleudy haearn bwrw yn Ewrop. Codwyd hwn yn 1865 i helpu atal llongddrylliadau ar y glannau peryglus hyn.

Above Ospreys arrive in the UK from Africa in late March/April, and stay until August/September

Right The cast iron Whiteford Lighthouse stands 44 metres (144 feet) tall and is the only wave-swept cast-iron tower of its size in Britain

The ospreys

Another exciting benefit of this new landscape has been the sighting of ospreys; a top predator, their presence indicates a good habitat. The Trust has erected a platform to attract adult osprey on their migratory flight to Africa in the hope that they will stop off here to nest and feed their young. Two bird hides have also been built to watch them and the other birds which populate, such as hen harriers, kingfishers and lapwings. *For more on Cwm Ivy and present day conservation on Gower, see page 62.*

Whiteford Lighthouse

Many ships have come to grief on Whiteford Sands, victims of the Atlantic Ocean's strong currents. Whiteford Lighthouse (not owned by the National Trust) was built in 1865 to help prevent such incidents. It is the only remaining sea-washed, cast-iron lighthouse in Europe and was last used during the Second World War to guide naval craft into Llanelli Dock and as target practice from the ranges at Crofty.

The lighthouse can be reached on foot at low tide, but be wary of the tide turning and of unexploded shells and mortars.

WALK THIS WAY

Llanmadoc Green to Berges Island Circular Walk
Goleudy, gorwelion a bywyd gwyllt

Take in some of the highlights of this area of Gower, including Cwm Ivy and the long stretch of Whiteford Sands.

- Moderate
- 2.5 hours at a leisurely pace
- 5 miles/8km
- Dog friendly

Terrain: Relatively flat, but mainly on loose sand and unsurfaced woodland paths. There is a steep lane at the start and end of the walk.

Mae disgrifiad Cymraeg o'r daith hon ar ein gwefan

Start: Llanmadoc Green

1. From Llanmadoc Green, follow the main road, bearing right just in front of St Madoc's Church. Follow the lane downhill, past the car park field on your right, to Cwm Ivy. At Cwm Ivy Court Farm, turn right through the National Trust gate signed Cwm Ivy. Follow the track down, but carry straight on when the track bears right to a gate, keeping the pine woods to your right. On your left is Cwm Ivy Tor, an inland limestone cliff that has gradually become separated from the sea by the moving sands that now form the dunes.

2. At the end of the track, bear right through the gate in to Whiteford Burrows NNR, and follow the sandy track through the dunes towards the sea. Turn right along the beach.

3. Continue walking along the beach for about 1½ miles (2.4km) towards Whiteford Lighthouse. At the end of the beach bear right, following the beach around the edge of the dunes.

4. A copse of conifers will come into view directly in front of you on a tiny peninsula known as Berges Island. This is a popular spot with birdwatchers, and egrets and ospreys have been spotted here.

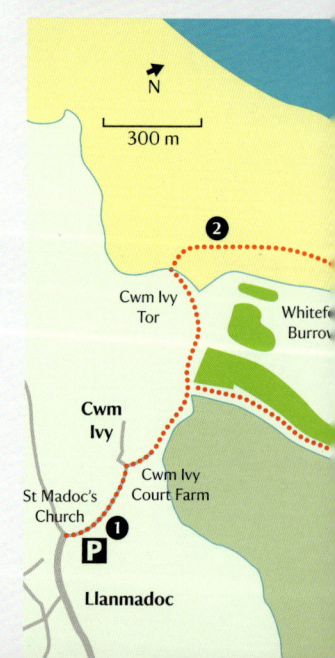

Top This walk takes you along the beach towards the ornate, Victorian Whiteford Lighthouse

56 TOURING THE COAST

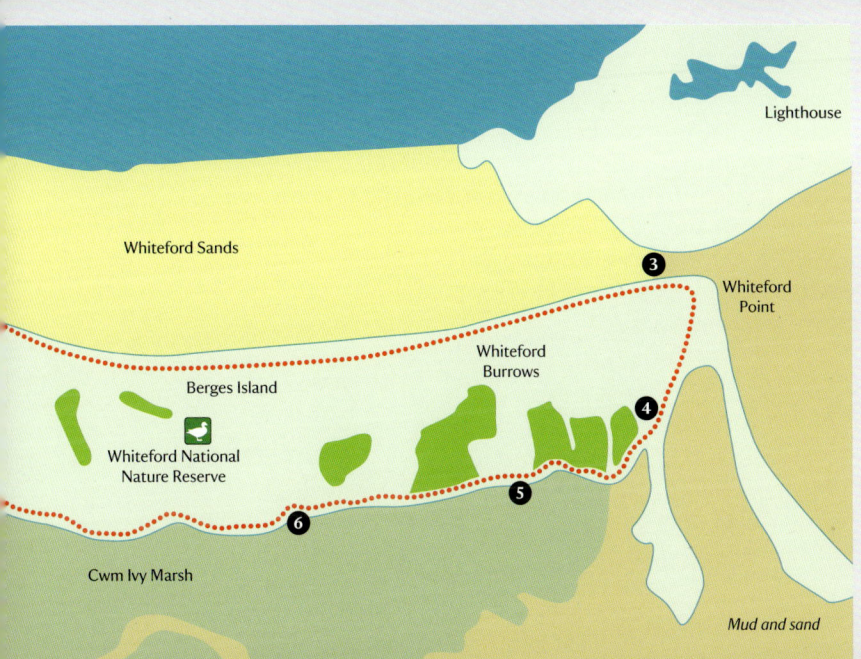

5. Before you reach Berges Island, there is a conifer plantation at the edge of the beach. When you are parallel with the far edge of the plantation, turn right off the beach, by the military warning sign, on to a narrow path into the woods. Where the path forks, keep left and follow it through the plantation until it eventually joins a track. Follow the track straight ahead. There are views over the saltmarsh to the left after leaving the plantation.

6. To complete the walk, go through the gate and bear left up the hill, retracing your steps back to the start.

TOURING THE COAST 57

The North Coast
Llanw, llaid a llonyddwch

Unlike the south, with its rocky coves and sandy beaches, Gower's north coast is a tranquil landscape of marshland, tussocky mudflats and tidal ditches.

Overlooking the Loughor Estuary (also known as the Burry Inlet) which divides Gower from the south coast of Carmarthenshire, the already extensive marsh increases in depth by a further four miles at low tide, revealing vast stretches of light-reflecting mud and sand.

The National Trust looks after most of this coastline, including the six miles of Llanrhidian Marsh (see page 60).

Local delicacies

While on the Gower, why not try a traditional Welsh breakfast of cockles served with laverbread (made from seaweed, also produced locally) coated in oatmeal and fried in bacon fat.

Saltmarsh lamb has a distinctive flavour, gained from the sheep grazing on marsh plants such as samphire and sorrel. Find it served in hotels and restaurants.

Above Llanrhidian Marsh

Right Turnstones like rocky, sandy and muddy shores

Far right The large, stocky oystercatcher mostly eats mussels and cockles when on the coast (inland they usually plump for worms)

piod môr **Llwchwr** cocos **cwtiad y traeth** bara lawr **cig oen** **morfa heli** Penclawdd **hocyswydden** corn carw'r môr **Llanrhidian** defaid **merlod** pibydd yr aber **llaid** cornchwiglen

✓ THINGS TO DO ON THE NORTH COAST

Bring some binoculars
Watch the wading birds pick out their food along the shoreline.

Go for a walk
Take to the Welsh coast path to enjoy this quiet and peaceful place.

Visit Penclawdd's food market
Held on Saturdays, this is the perfect place to stock up on local produce.

👁 LOOK OUT FOR

Marsh plants
Horsetail, marsh mallow and sea rush grow below the sea wall on the edge of Llanrhidian Marsh.

Wading birds
Golden plovers, knots, lapwings, oystercatchers and turnstones can be seen searching for food on the mudflats.

Llanrhidian Marsh and the estuary
Patrymau cain, straeon cudd

Sŵn gwaith copr, pres, tun a glo oedd yn atseinio ar hyd y glannau hyn yn y 19egG. Mae'r arfer o hel cocos yn yr aber yn parhau, ond tractorau yn hytrach nag asynnod sy'n cludo'r llwythi nôl i'r tir mawr erbyn hyn. Mae'r merlod a'r defaid sy'n pori'r morfa wedi hen arfer â'r llanw slei ac mae'r heli yn rhoi blas arbennig i'r cig oen o'r ardal hon.

Designated as both a Special Area of Conservation and SSSI, the Marsh is an important habitat for wading and over-wintering birds, which can be seen in considerable numbers feeding on the abundance of crabs, molluscs and worms.

The Marsh is common land which means that farmers have ancient rights to graze their animals here, mainly sheep which are moved inland when high spring tides race in and submerge the area. The saltmarsh lamb that is produced as a result is a local delicacy. *For more on commons, see page 18.*

Wild ponies roam the estuary, feeding on gorse and tough grasses and keeping the invasion of unwelcome species at bay by trampling on them. They are unbowed by the rising tide and stay put with the sea lapping around their bellies until it retreats.

This is a place of gentle, reflective beauty, a vital resource for wildlife and plant species and a lovely place to wander, watch the birds, discover rare marshland plant species and enjoy the big skies and wide horizons.

An industrious past
But the north coast has not always been so peaceful: Penclawdd has a rich industrial heritage – up until the end of the 19th century, it had a coal mine and tinplate, copper and brass works, plus a railway station and 11 pubs. It was also the centre for cockling, an activity that continues today.

Warming the cockles
The mudflats near Penclawdd are rich with cockles, which have been harvested here since Roman times. Gathering cockles is back-breaking work. For centuries it was undertaken by women (the men worked in the mines and collieries) who scraped at the sand to reveal the cockles, then raked them into piles before sieving them in riddles to separate the largest ones. Donkeys laden with wicker baskets carried the haul to market. Today cockles remain hand gathered, but the donkeys have been replaced by tractors. Although they are mostly exported to Europe, you can buy Gower cockles locally at markets and online.

Bove Hill
One of the best places to see the sweep of Llanrhidian Marsh and the north Gower coastline is from the top of Bove Hill. This small area, which is on a public right of way, not only has great views but also boasts a variety of habitats including ash woodland, grassy heath and limestone outcrops.

The National Trust usually relies on grazing animals to keep down scrub and allow wildflowers to flourish, but this is common land and so cannot be fenced. Instead, volunteers help us to keep the blackthorn and bramble at bay and so boost biodiversity.

Left The peaceful expanse of Llanrhidian Marsh

Above Penclawdd cocklewomen with their donkeys

Looking after Gower
Gofalu am Fro Gŵyr

Owning three quarters of the Gower coastline comes with responsibilities.

As custodian, the National Trust takes this responsibility seriously. Our rangers and staff work with volunteers – some full time, some on working holidays, others who have given up a day or two – all-year round to manage and conserve this precious place.

The changing coastline and Cwm Ivy

Coastal and climate change is unpredictable and can be devastating. To counter this, the Trust has developed a long-term plan to work with nature rather than against it.

In November 2013, the medieval wall which had kept the sea at bay at Cwm Ivy for centuries began to look shaky. Persistent heavy rain caused an inland stream to swell to such an extent that the marsh was not able to drain. Storms, tidal surges and high tides caused further battering until, in August 2014, the wall was breached. But rather than repair it, we let the sea come in.

Now the land is returning to what it was before the wall: a species-rich saltmarsh. Four months after the tide re-covered the marsh, the first saltmarsh seedlings – glasswort and sea spurry – began to grow. It is like a plant nursery as more seeds lodge and take root.

Here are the marks of feeding shoals of grey mullet, which came in on the tide, and rasped the surface layer of algae. Reed beds have sprung from nowhere, providing habitats for bittern and water voles. From our two bird hides, a wealth of birds can be spotted, including curlews, kingfishers, lapwings, little egrets and marsh harriers. Dragonflies, grass snakes and otters also call Cwm Ivy home.

The future

The return of the saltmarsh at Cwm Ivy is one of the biggest coastal realignment projects in Wales. From now on, rather than maintaining the sea wall, our efforts will be spent on managing the change from freshwater marsh to saltmarsh. We will simply monitor what happens with as little intervention as possible. By allowing nature to come back in, the coastal habitat is being restored to its natural state.

Above The breached medieval sea wall at Cwm Ivy

Top right Otters can sometimes be spotted in Cwm Ivy marsh

Right Storm damage at Rhossili, caused during the storms of 2014

Managing Rhossili

The way we manage access to the beach at Rhossili has also altered in the last few years after serious erosion following the winter storms of 2014. The path used to finish with concrete and stone steps to the beach but these were washed away and were almost impossible to re-build in the same location. We opted instead for a sloped footpath to the beach which will be simple and quick to move and repair if damaged by storms in the future.

Mae Penrhyn Gŵyr yn newid drwy'r amser ac mae'n bwysig gweithio gyda grymoedd natur yn lle brwydro'n barhaus. Dyma pam ein bod ni'n gadael i'r môr orlifo'r tir yng Nghwm Ivy a throi'r cynefin yn ôl yn forfa heli cyfoethog, a pham hefyd ein bod ni'n ail-gynllunio llwybr at y traeth yn Rhosili fel y bydd hi'n haws i'w adnewyddu ar ôl stormydd yn y dyfodol.

Plans for the future
Dyfodol disglair

Although there is already a rich diversity of habitat on Gower, we have a five-year plan in place to increase it.

This involves clearing the gorse on the South Gower coast, which will allow other species to grow and keeps down the risk of fire from dry gorse bushes. Other invasive plants such as brambles and cotoneaster need to be strimmed to control them, too. We also clear areas to create corridors for insects and butterflies – one of these 'rides' is behind Burrows Cottage, near Whiteford Burrows – and alter the way the site is grazed to encourage more dune flowering plants to flourish. Whiteford is already good for butterflies such as the marbled white and dark green fritillary, so more flowers will serve to increase this.

Planting and growing
It's not all about clearing; we grow things as well. Native hedges are laid, young trees are planted and we are boosting the wild asparagus population – a nationally scarce species – by growing new plants from seed collected from wild plants on Gower. These are cultivated for five years before they are brought back and re-introduced.

A helping hand
You will also see with us our trusty band of volunteers, litter picking on beaches and building new fences. There is never a shortage of things to do!

Mae gennym gynllun pum mlynedd cynhyrfus ar gyfer Penrhyn Gŵyr. Dewch i'n helpu ni i greu cynefinoedd gwych ar gyfer byd natur. O glirio eithin a phlanhigion ymledol i addasu'r patrymau pori ar gyfer glöynnod byw, ac o dyfu ac ail-blannu planhigion prin i adfer gwrychoedd a choedwigoedd – mae 'na ddigon i'w wneud bob amser!

Above Volunteers carrying out an otter territory survey at Cwm Ivy